"We must

be the

change

we want

to see in

the world."

— Mahatma
Gandhi

WALKTHETALK.COM

Resources for Personal and Professional Success

Helping Individuals and Organizations
Achieve Success Through Values-Based Practices

Ouch! That Stereotype Hurts

Inquiries regarding permission for use of the material contained in this book should be addressed to:
        The WALK THE TALK Company
        1100 Parker Square, Suite 250
        Flower Mound, TX 75028
        972.899.8300

WALK THE TALK books may be purchased for educational, business, or sales promotion use.

WALK THE TALK® and The WALK THE TALK® Company are registered trademarks of
Performance Systems Corporation.

Printed in the United States of America
10 9 8 7 6 5 4 3

Edited by Steve Ventura and Michelle Sedas
Designed by Branch-Smith
Printed by MultiAd

ISBN 1-885228-72-4

9 781885 228727   90000

Ouch!

That Stereotype Hurts

COMMUNICATING RESPECTFULLY IN A DIVERSE WORLD

LESLIE C. AGUILAR

Communicating

Respectfully in

a Diverse

World

Table of Contents

Continued on next page

Acknowledgement

This book is dedicated to Joel Marks, who sees endless possibilities and then makes them happen. Thank you, Joel, for your thought partnership during the writing of *Ouch! That Stereotype Hurts*.

I'm grateful to the individuals who first encouraged me to do this work – Jo Lamb, Bill MacKellar-Hertan, and Ruth Bond – and to the thousands of participants who have explored this topic with me in *Inclusive Communication* workshops over the last ten years. Your experiences and questions have helped to define and evolve the skills and techniques included in these pages. I've been inspired by your many stories and the courage with which you have spoken up against bias and stereotypes.

Thank you, Robin Heath, for first introducing me to the "Ouch!" technique. Thank you, Dr. Robin Johnson, for your passion and insight on bias-free communication.

I would like to give credit to a book that informed me, influenced me and drew me into this topic. It is *Without Bias: A Guidebook for Nondiscriminatory Communication* edited by Judy E. Pickens and published by the International Association of Business Communicators in 1982. While *Without Bias* is no longer in print, its message remains important today. It helped shape some of the guidelines you will find in *Ouch! That Stereotype Hurts*.

I am also indebted to a complete stranger – the disk jockey at a party – who showed me the power of a sole voice speaking up on behalf of respect. I will share his story in this book.

While we may

never be

completely free

of all bias,

we *can*

work toward

communicating

in bias-free

ways.

Introduction

We All Communicate

Think that communication is only for communication departments? Think again. Everyone communicates. Whether you are a team leader, team member, educator, machine operator, supervisor, executive, customer service rep, or accountant, you need to communicate with other people to be successful in your job.

Think your communication is always bias-free? Think that you are equally respectful and effective with a "diverse" range of people – people who are similar to you and people who are different? These are tougher questions and the true answers may surprise you. Chances are very high your communication has some degree of bias in it. Occasionally, you may send messages that some people are valued and some are not. And, there's a good chance you sometimes exclude or stereotype people, even though you don't intend to.

The fact is – people are naturally biased. Not only "those people over there," but also you and me. And we have a tendency to let some of our biases slip into communication, consciously or unconsciously. When that happens, everyone loses. Relationships suffer. Cooperation decreases. Your ability to lead or influence others diminishes. Those who feel demeaned and excluded often "drop out." They stop listening. They may even stop respecting you. The result: All too frequently, your intended message never gets through. Not good!

Biased, stereotypical, or otherwise demeaning communication also undermines morale, teamwork, and productivity in your organization. It can drive customers away. It can cause a public relations fiasco. And, it could be interpreted as an indicator of a hostile workplace – exposing you to the nightmare of legal action. Even if you never have a lawsuit, bias and stereotyping certainly do *not* contribute to an environment where employees can do their best work.

The great news is that each of us can choose to communicate more effectively. We can identify our own biases, explore ways to reduce them, and work to communicate in more inclusive, bias-free ways. That's what this book is about.

Ouch! That Stereotype Hurts will help you:

- Improve your written and verbal communication by eliminating communication "static."

- Ensure your message gets across – while conveying respect for others.

- Gain insight into the impact of your language choices.

- Learn ways to successfully recover when you've put your foot in your mouth.

- Speak up effectively if others stereotype or make biased or demeaning comments.

- Enhance your credibility and influence as a communicator.

Whether you are coming from the head – looking for practical tips and proven techniques – or from the heart – understanding and sincerely caring about how you affect others – use this book to help you be the communicator you want and need to be.

Isn't This Just P.C.?

I'm sometimes asked if paying close attention to one's words and nonverbal communication is simply being "Politically Correct." My answer: "No, it's about a *different* 'P.C.' It's about being 'Professionally Competent'... being 'Personally Conscious.'" And, it's about *respect.* Bias-free, inclusive communication is both professional and humane – both competent and caring – and helps the message reach a diverse range of listeners.

What Is Bias?

Bias means a *predisposition* to see things or people in a certain way. You can be biased toward some people and predisposed to see them in a positive light. Likewise, you can be predisposed to see others in a negative light, based on their appearance, group kinships, or differences from you.

Bias is an *internal* belief. It is a *mental prejudgment*, positive or negative, made about an individual. It's not until you act it out in speech and behavior that others receive the impact. Consider the potential effects of the following words and actions:

- The team leader who says: *"Let Jen work the holiday. She's single; she doesn't have a family."* Effects: discounting (treating as less valuable), unfair treatment of single employees

- The colleague who demonstrates interest or respect only to people in management, while ignoring or talking down to entry-level employees. Effects: discounting of entry-level staff, "us versus them" divisions between management and employees, communication breakdowns

- The manager who hires only young, "attractive" females for customer service roles. Effects: potential mismatch of talent and job, discrimination against other equally or more qualified candidates

- The sales associate who treats shoppers of other races or ethnic groups with suspicion, watching them as if they were shoplifters. Effects: poor customer service, lost sales, potential discrimination

- The executive who unknowingly schedules the department retreat on Yom Kippur and, when told of this, says, *"Well, unfortunately, we'll have to keep that date – it's the only good day available."* Effects: exclusion of employees, loss of team cohesion

The message embedded in all of these examples is that some humans are inherently less valuable, less worthwhile, somehow less deserving of human dignity than others. These types of biased words and actions add unnecessary distractions or static to the message. Over and above impeding clear communication, bias can result in loss of speaker credibility, low employee morale and teamwork, poor customer service and sales, turnover of employees, unfair treatment of others, and discrimination. That's why it is important to recognize and eliminate biased words and behaviors.

Communicating Respect and Inclusion

While we may never be completely free of all bias, we *can* work toward communicating in bias-free ways that are most likely to respect and include the listener. The following pages will show you how.

In Chapter One you will gain insight into the ways you may unintentionally convey bias or exclusion in your written or spoken message. You will explore guidelines to help you achieve bias-free communication. Chapter Two will show you what to do when things go wrong – when you have mistakenly said something demeaning and your foot is in your mouth. In Chapter Three you will learn twelve techniques for speaking up against bias and stereotypes without blame or guilt. And, in Chapter Four you'll discover how advance planning can help ensure that you communicate respect and inclusion (being a valued member of the group).

Throughout *Ouch! That Stereotype Hurts,* you will find many practical models, strategies, and examples that you can apply to enhance your communication success in a diverse world. In doing so, you will also help create a workplace where *all* individuals are treated with respect and are able to do their best work.

Chapter One

The Language of Inclusion

"Communication provides the legs for bias,

carrying it from person to person,

from generation to generation.

Eventually, however, communication

will be the way to end discrimination."

– John N. Bailey, Past President,

International Association of Business Communicators

Without Bias: A Guidebook for Nondiscriminatory Communication

Have you ever heard others make biased, stereotypical, or unfair statements? Chances are the answer is *"yes."* If you've ever been the target of such statements, you know they sometimes cut deep. They can derail effective communication and relationship building.

We hear others being biased and unfair, yet most of us think we ourselves present information and lead discussions in ways that include everyone and avoid bias, stereotyping, and discounting. But far too often we unintentionally communicate bias and exclusion through words and actions. This adds unnecessary static to the message and makes it harder for listeners to receive the intended meaning.

To get you thinking about your own communication, complete the self-assessment that follows. Concentrate on your written communication at work. Ask yourself...

Self-Assessment

	Yes	No
Do I check my spelling on written communication?		
Do I have tools to help me do so, such as a dictionary, computer spell check, or friends who are great spellers?		
Do I ever reference a thesaurus to get just the right word?		
Do I keep a thesaurus close by or know where to find one?		
Do I proof my work to look for typos or incorrect grammar?		
Do I ever ask someone else to double check for typos or mistakes?		
Do I ever get irritated at others who send out memos / info with typos or errors?		
Do I have a "red pen" in my mind (or hand) with which I circle the typos?		
Do I complete a "bias check" on my communication?		
Do I have tools to help me check for stereotypes, discounting, and bias?		

Ninety percent of individuals who have taken this informal assessment in business settings have responded *"yes"* to each question until reaching *"Do I complete a 'bias check' on my communication?"* Fewer than ten percent of individuals communicating in the workplace consciously check their written communication for bias, stereotypes, and discounting.

I would suggest that it is equally as important – if not more important – to complete a bias check as it is to look for typos or missing commas or misspelled words. While grammatical errors will distract some readers and may be interpreted as a sign of carelessness, the effects of bias, exclusion, and discounting reach much further. They can distract, hurt, insult, anger or turn off the recipient, and damage your chances of communicating effectively.

This chapter will demonstrate "The Language of Inclusion" – how you can communicate in ways that include and involve everyone and avoid stereotyping, bias, and discounting. You will find tips, guidelines, and resources to help you get your written or verbal message across – effectively and with respect – in a diverse world.

"You Know How They Are" – Stereotypes

We're all familiar with stereotypes – they are simplified, fixed beliefs about a group of people. Most of us can quickly call to mind stereotypes about lots of groups. Think for a moment about the stereotypes you have heard expressed about older people, teenagers, Jews, Muslims, Christians, women, black men, white men, blondes (blonde women that is), overweight people, welfare recipients, rich people, lawyers, politicians, New Yorkers, or vegetarians. There's no doubt stereotypes exist in our society.

The Effects of Stereotyping

Many of the negative stereotypes are brutal. What may surprise you is that even so-called positive stereotypes can have a negative impact.

Consider these…

"Asians are good in math."

"African Americans are good at sports."

"Men are good leaders."

"Women are good nurturers."

Stereotyping affects both the person who holds the stereotype and the person being stereotyped. By seeing all people in a group as the same, you deny people their individuality. If you apply fixed beliefs about a group to an individual, you distort your ability to get a clear view of that person. This may lead you to prejudge or misjudge others.

If you have ever been stereotyped, you know it is often demeaning and offensive. If others treat you as less valuable or limit your opportunities based on negative preconceptions about "your group," it can have serious consequences on your life.

This is true even with the positive stereotypes. Imagine being the Asian-American student who loves marketing, yet the guidance counselor steers you to accounting, based on the counselor's beliefs that Asians are good in math.

Scenario: Unintended Consequences

Eight weeks after the birth of her baby, Mary returned to work. On her first day back in the office, she attended the division staff meeting. As the meeting convened, one of Mary's managers, Pat, called out:

"Wait, Wait! Before we get started, I'd like to welcome Mary back. Mary, congratulations on your new baby! We missed you and we're so happy to have you back…particularly since most women don't come back to work after having children."

People shifted in their seats. They looked at Mary, Pat, and at one another. Some looked down. No one spoke up. The general manager started the meeting: *"Welcome everyone. Here is our agenda for today…"*

Later, as people were leaving, you could hear their conversations in the hallway:

"Can you believe what Pat said?"
"I bet Mary was embarrassed."
"I wanted to say something, but I didn't know what to say."
"So, is that how they feel around this place?"
"What about me? I have three children, and I'm here."

This real-life situation shows how easily stereotypes can slip into conversation and how they undermine communication and relationships. Pat's intended message of warmth and welcome was lost – overshadowed by the stereotypical statement that followed. Everyone present was negatively affected, including Pat. Pat's statement stayed in people's minds throughout the meeting and for weeks after.

How to Recognize Stereotypes

In our society stereotyping is prevalent. The key is this – become cognizant of stereotypes when they occur so you can make conscious choices about how to address them.

Some stereotypes are blatant, such as *"They all look the same"* or *"They are all _____."* Most stereotypes surface in more subtle ways. They may be mixed in with other information and passed off as facts. They may be "just a joke." Regardless of the packaging, stereotypes are all based on the same thought process that clumps individuals together as members of a group, with no acknowledgement of individual differences.

Stereotypes typically have three characteristics:

1) They imply that *all* people in the group are the same.

   "You know how men are."

2) They contain a *judgment*. Notice that the judgment often reveals more about the stereotyp<u>er's</u> beliefs or expectations than it does about the stereotyp<u>ed</u> individual.

   "Young people today don't have a good work ethic."

   This reflects the mindset of the stereotyp<u>er</u> – everyone should structure work the same way he or she does. It does not acknowledge that many younger people work very hard, or that there are different ways to accomplish meaningful work.

3) Stereotypes are fairly *inflexible*. When we encounter someone who does not fit our stereotype, it's easier to consider that person the "exception to the rule," rather than question the validity of the stereotype.

   I met an engineer at a large national conference who was a good-looking, dark-skinned man from the Caribbean. In the few minutes that we sat together, two people who were introduced commented: *"You don't look like an engineer."*

Even if you personally try to avoid using them, you may still occasionally slip into stereotypes. And you *will* encounter them in the workplace and in society. In order to deal with stereotypes, you must first be able to recognize them when they occur.

Following is a tool that makes recognizing the subtle and not-so-subtle stereotypes easier. The left column identifies common ways stereotypes are packaged. On the right are examples of each type of stereotype. As you scan the list, notice if you have ever heard similar kinds of stereotypes about various groups.

EIGHT COMMON WAYS STEREOTYPES SURFACE AND ARE PERPETUATED

1) Jokes	*"Do you know what happens when you get three _____ together?"*
2) Name-Calling/Labels	*"Blue Hair"* • *"Computer Geek"* • *"Trailer Trash"*
3) Oversimplified Statements Applied to ALL People in a Group	*"Young workers today _____."* • *"Immigrants don't want to learn English."* • *"Latinos are _____."* • *"You know how Southerners are."*
4) Stereotypical Descriptors	*"Crotchety old man"* • *"Women are very emotional."* • *"Typical white male"*
5) Personal Assumptions About Individuals (based on stereotypes held about a group the individual is a member of)	Assuming a woman's career is secondary to family. Therefore, not offering a career opportunity to a woman that would require her to relocate her family. • Assuming front-line employees don't have the skill sets for a special assignment, and therefore not considering any front-line employees.

6) Spokesperson Syndrome	Viewing one individual as the spokesperson for an entire group. *"Marta, what is the best way to deal with the Hispanic market?"* • *"Glenn, what do black people think about this?"* Identifying an individual from a minority group as a "community leader" if he or she speaks up on an issue (i.e., in the media).
7) Descriptors That Evoke Stereotypes Because They Are the Opposite or a Contradiction to an Existing Stereotype	*"We're looking for qualified minority candidates."* • *"A sensitive man"*
8) "Statistical" Stereotyping	*"Statistics show that most criminals are _____."* Then treating an individual based on the "statistic." Note: The statistic could be real or perceived.
• • • • • • • • • • • • • • • • • • •	• •
Note: Stereotypes are so powerful that often we hold on to them even when evidence disproves the stereotype.	*"You don't look like a(n) _____."* • *"You're not like most _____."* • *"She's really articulate for a(n) _____."*

Your Choice: Moving Past Stereotypes

Moving past stereotypes requires a conscious choice to treat people as individuals rather than as members of a set – to interrupt stereotypes rather than perpetuate them. In a society where stereotypes abound, this takes vigilance to identify and energy to address.

Guidelines for Stereotype-Free Communication

Here are some guidelines for eliminating stereotypes from your communication.

Individualize: Treat people as individuals rather than as members of a set.

Avoid Stereotypical Jokes and Humor: They are often demeaning and embarrassing to listeners.

Use Accurate Descriptions: Replace descriptors, clichés, and labels that rely on stereotypes with specific, accurate, and relevant words. *"She reminds you when work is overdue"* is more specific and less stereotypical than *"She's a nag."*

Depict People Non-Stereotypically in Visuals: When using graphics or visuals, ensure that the images do not reinforce stereotypes. For example, use photographs depicting role models that include people of different ages, ethnicities, physical abilities, body sizes, and genders.

Check for Assumptions: Many assumptions about individuals are based on stereotypes held about a group the individual is part of. Interrupt, question, and examine all assumptions. Instead of assuming that Sondra doesn't want a job that requires longer hours because of her medical condition, ask her: *"Sondra, here are the requirements of the job… Are you interested?"*

Solicit Multiple Opinions: If you are seeking information about a group of people, seek input from multiple sources. Avoid expecting one person to be a "spokesperson" for all members of a group simply because she or he is a member of the group. You could say: *"Marta, Mario, Adriana, what are your opinions of this product? What about you, Carlos?"*

When you are talking with Marta, Mario, Adriana, Carlos, and others, you could also ask questions such as *"How do you think others would feel about this product?"*

Or, more specifically, *"I'm trying to better understand how this product might be received in the Hispanic community. What is your perception of how other Latinos might feel about this product?"*

Learn the Hot Spots: Be sensitive to common negative stereotypes about groups. This will help you understand strong reactions to a seemingly positive description. For instance, a person described as *"poor but hard-working"* may feel the sting of the unspoken stereotype that people are poor because they are lazy. How do you find out what the hot spots are? Listen! Observe! Ask! Friends or coworkers will likely tell you what stereotypes bother them, if you ask.

Interrupt Stereotypes: When stereotypes surface in your own or others' decisions, words, and actions, question them rather than repeat or act on them. How do you interrupt stereotypes? You will find effective and respectful techniques in Chapter Three.

Inclusive Language – Who Is Included? Excluded?

When you are trying to get your message across to a broad audience, you need to use language that includes and demonstrates respect for *everyone*. The words you choose send messages about who is included, and who is not. An obvious example is gender language. Gender-inclusive language seeks to eliminate stereotyping, to promote equitable treatment for men and women, and to include, rather than exclude, listeners based on gender. Consider the following statement:

> *"A good leader understands his strengths and weaknesses. This applies to all professions — whether you are a policeman, a fireman, a teacher, a salesman, or even the CEO or Chairman of the Board."*

What do you think? Does this statement include men? women? both? How do you know? I've asked this of thousands of participants in the training room. All easily agree that men are included. There is confusion and disagreement about whether women are included or not. This is unneeded static in the communication.

There are times that you will want to communicate to men only or women only. Other times you'll want to communicate to *everyone*, with no confusion about whether both men and women are included. When you want to send a message that includes everyone, you have a choice to use language that is inclusive of all people. Here are some helpful guidelines.

Guidelines for Gender-Inclusive Language

<u>Use Inclusive Terms:</u> When you wish to clearly communicate to both men and women, use language that refers to both. Here are four different techniques to make the following phrase more gender-inclusive.

"When I meet an executive, I wonder what his leadership style is like."

1) Use both pronouns: *"When I meet an executive, I wonder what his or her leadership style is like."*

2) Use the plural form: *"When I meet executives, I wonder what their leadership styles are like."*

3) Reword: *"I'm interested in the different leadership styles of the executives I meet."*

4) Vary your statements – at times refer to executives as males (he / him) and, at times, as females (she / her).

<u>Use Inclusive Titles:</u> Avoid titles that indicate the job is normally performed by one sex (*i.e., Policeman*). Utilize gender-neutral titles (*i.e., Police Officer*) unless you specifically want to emphasize one or both genders (*i.e., "Policemen and Policewomen"*).

Identify Gender Only When Relevant: Typically there's no need to refer to a doctor as *"a lady doctor"* or to a nurse as *"a male nurse."* There are times, however, when gender *is* relevant and should be included, such as when you are describing what a person in a crowd looks like or when discussing men's issues or women's issues.

Use Titles Equally: Use parallel titles and salutations for both genders, such as *"John McCain and Hillary Clinton"* or *"Senator John McCain and Senator Hillary Clinton."* Avoid disparate treatment such as *"Senators McCain and Hillary."*

Broaden References: Use a broad range of stories, examples, analogies, and role models that appeal to different interests (e.g., sports, history, gardening, music, dance, literature, parenting). This is more likely to reach a broad audience than using only sports examples.

Naming and Describing People – Images Evoked

Language has power. Based on the way you choose to name and describe people, you send different messages. For instance, what images are evoked in your mind when you hear *"A cancer victim,"* *"A person suffering from cancer,"* or *"A person with cancer"*? Where is your attention drawn in each of these two phrases: *"The disabled employee speaks three languages"* versus *"The employee speaks three languages"*?

Naming, identifying, or describing people can sometimes be awkward. Some communicators are so uncomfortable that they steer away from discussing important topics such as race, gender, religion, disabilities, or sexual orientation. This is unfortunate! We can't be clear and precise in our communication if we're walking on eggshells. Even more importantly, if we want to learn from one another and be respectful of one another we will sometimes need to discuss age, religious practices, gender, or other similarities and differences among us.

So how *can* you describe people without being offensive? You start with good intent. Then you choose language you feel *is most likely* to convey respect and inclusion. The good and bad news is this – there is no one right way. There are, however, guidelines that can help.

Guidelines for Naming or Describing People

<u>Eliminate Overt Disrespect</u>: The easiest way to demonstrate respect when describing people is to purge obviously derogatory terms from your vocabulary. There are some descriptors that are clearly considered demeaning by large numbers of people. They are the terms that before saying them, people look around first to see who is in the room. They are the terms that are referred to as letters … the "N-word," the "B-word." They are the terms that are used in anger to berate or humiliate someone. Don't use these words – even if some have lost their power due to common use or passage of time. Don't say them, even in jest; Even if you heard them in your favorite song; Even if your best friend uses them. Don't use them in professional, respectful communication.

<u>Allow Self-Determination</u>: People decide what they want to be called. The only "correct" term for individuals or groups of people is that which they choose for themselves. One way to demonstrate respect for others is to refer to them in ways that *they* find meaningful. How do you know how people describe themselves? Listen! Read! Refer to a bias-free word finder or dictionary. Notice the names of associations, chambers, and other organizations. Ask! Of course, not everyone in a group will agree due to individual or regional differences. There may be multiple respectful terms (e.g., *Latino, Hispanic, or more specifically, Mexican-American, or Puerto Rican*). And, some individuals will tell you they prefer to be called by their name, with no descriptors.

<u>Put People First, Qualifiers Second</u>: Mention the person *first*, and let qualifiers follow, *only* when they are relevant. For example, there's no need to point out the accountant's wheelchair unless the conversation is specifically about his or her disability. In that case, a respectful "people-first" phrase is: *"The accountant uses a wheelchair…"* rather than *"the disabled accountant."*

Avoid Patronizing Language: Don't use terms that diminish individuals, even if you don't personally feel any "charge" from the word (e.g., describing individuals with disabilities or medical conditions as *"pitiful,"* *"helpless,"* or *"suffering,"* or children from single-parent families as coming from *"broken homes")*. Likewise, avoid ascribing "superhuman" characteristics such as *"heroic,"* *"courageous,"* or *"amazing"* to someone with a disability who accomplishes everyday tasks such as arriving at work on time. This is equally condescending – it conveys your surprise that this person is as capable or committed as others are.

Grant Equal Status: Use parallel terms when talking about two groups. Try to describe people by who they are, rather than who they are not. Statements like *"White and Non-White"* and *"Management and Non-Management"* position one group as the "norm" and others as the "non-norm." Instead, consider using *"people of all ethnic and racial groups"* and *"Management and Staff."*

Recognize Insider / Outsider Dynamics: Don't use "us versus them" language, such as *"you people."* It's divisive. Also, even if some people within a group use offensive language about themselves, that doesn't make it OK for you to use. It's demeaning and often even more highly charged if stated by an outsider.

Use Precise and Specific Descriptors: Remember, there is no need to point out disability, gender, ethnicity, age, or sexual orientation when it is not pertinent to the conversation. However, when they *are* relevant, don't avoid important descriptors. You have the option between vague, general language and precise, specific language. Choose precise language. This allows people to feel they are being described accurately and not clumped into large generic groups. It also leads to clearer communication. For example, *"Vietnamese"* is more specific than *"Asian."* *"He has a visual impairment"* is more informative than *"He has a disability."*

The "Turn-Around Test"

When in doubt about whether you are being respectful, bias-free, and non-stereotypical in your descriptions of others, apply the "Turn-Around Test." To use this tool, replace the individual or group you are describing with a different person or group. If your description now sounds absurd, insensitive, or inappropriate, there's a good chance your original statement was stereotypical or otherwise biased. While this doesn't work 100% of the time, it causes you to examine your thought process, which is always helpful. Here are some examples.

If you describe a female politician by how well she can (or can't) cook, would you also describe a male politician by how well he cooks? The Turn-Around Test shows that the cooking reference is probably gender-based, and not relevant to the conversation at hand.

A media headline stated: *"Blacks in America Can't Agree on a Solution."* Consider the Turn-Around phrase: *"Whites in America Can't Agree on a Solution."* By examining these two statements, you find the stereotypical thinking that all people in a racial group think the same.

You may recall the Native-American author who used the Turn-Around Test in response to the question of why naming sports teams *"Indians," "Redskins,"* or *"Braves"* is considered offensive. He said to imagine naming a team the *"Brooklyn Jews"* or the *"Los Angeles Negroes"* and then creating a mascot for the team. The name choice is insensitive and the mascots can perpetuate stereotypes.

Jokes and Humor

Humor is important! It is a powerful communication tool. It helps us relax, release stress, and enjoy life and work. However, a lot of humor is based on degrading or stereotyping others. To repeat the stereotype, even if it's "just a joke," perpetuates it – gives it legs to walk to the next person.

Destructive humor in the workplace also affects the joke teller. Stereotypical and demeaning jokes are often interpreted by listeners as a sign that the communicator is unprofessional, bigoted, or insensitive. That's definitely not helpful if you are trying to improve your communication skills or your credibility.

Guidelines for Inclusive and Respectful Humor

Choose Positive Humor: Laugh at yourself and your own personal foibles. Share funny stories about what happened to you or others – based on the comedy of the situation. Just make sure your jokes, stories, or e-mails don't stereotype or demean individuals or groups based on who they are (e.g., their race, accent, or appearance).

Cull Your Humor "File": Keep the funny, non-disparaging jokes, plays on words, cartoons, stories, and images. Pass these on. Delete the ones that demean or debase people.

Apply the "Humor Test": Ask yourself: *"Is it professional?" "Is it respectful?" "Does it avoid perpetuating stereotypes?"* If all three answers are *"yes,"* then it's probably a safe bet for the workplace.

Nonverbal Messages

We cannot end this chapter without acknowledging nonverbal behavior. Gestures, facial expressions, and voice tone also communicate inclusion or exclusion, respect or disrespect.

A leader standing in front of the meeting hall says, *"We value every member of the team from the CEO* (hand held up high), *all the way to the customer service rep,"* (while dropping the hand down to thigh level). The leader has given a very powerful message. Some people are valued, and some are at the bottom of the heap.

The colleague who says she values you but only makes eye contact in meetings with higher-ups in the company is giving you two conflicting messages. The words say, *"I value you."* The nonverbal message says, *"You don't matter."* Which do you believe – the words or the actions?

Usually, when spoken and unspoken messages contradict each other, we perceive the nonverbal message as true. So, as you work to eliminate bias from your communication, focus also on what you "say" nonverbally.

Summary

Speaking the Language of Inclusion is one way to demonstrate respect for your listeners. It means choosing language and nonverbal communication that includes everyone and avoids bias, stereotyping, and discounting. This eliminates unnecessary static from your communication and makes it more likely that your message can get across to a broad range of people.

There is no list of what to say or do that will guarantee you are inclusive and bias-free in your communication. Through respectful intention and positive word choice, however, you can...

- Communicate clearly

- Avoid stereotyping and discounting of others

- Help people feel they are included in your message

- Name and describe people in ways that are accurate, unbiased, and relevant

- Select jokes and humor that celebrate our common humanity rather than demean one another for our differences.

When you consistently demonstrate respect and inclusion, others will be more willing to forgive you if you occasionally "slip up" and mistakenly communicate bias. While bias-free communication takes ongoing effort, it will help you build a foundation of trust with your listeners.

So, next time you reach for a dictionary, thesaurus, or spell check, think about checking for stereotypes and bias as well.

Communication

Recovery is an

underutilized skill.

The good news is —

it's not that

difficult to do,

and it has

a big payoff.

Chapter Two

Communication Recovery –

What to Do When Things Go Wrong

"If you want to get out of the pit,

stop digging."

– Ernesto Santos-DeJesus

University of Maryland University College

Have you ever said something unintentionally offensive and wished you could take it back? If so, you know how awkward it feels when communication goes awry. And it does from time to time. Even with the best of intent to be inclusive, you might say something biased, stereotypical, or exclusionary. You can choose to ignore it and hope no one notices. (Guess what – it was noticed!) Or, you can employ a strategy for recovery.

"Communication Recovery" involves acknowledging your mistake, sincerely apologizing, and then moving on in a more inclusive way. Communication Recovery is an underutilized skill. When things go wrong in communication, many people shy away from trying to recover. They are afraid of making things worse. They don't know what to do. The good news is Communication Recovery is possible, it's not that difficult to do, and it has a big payoff.

It's a lot like "Service Recovery." If you are in business and you make a service mistake, you have to fix it or the customer goes away unhappy and tells everyone what a bad experience he or she had.

You've probably experienced this yourself as a customer. Have you ever received a meal that was undercooked or burnt? If you asked to have it corrected and the server treated you rudely, think about how you responded. How many people did you tell about your bad experience? Most people tell at least nine others. Were you willing to go to that restaurant again? Many people aren't.

What if, on the other hand, the server said, "*I am so sorry – let me fix that. And while you are waiting let me bring you a complimentary appetizer to hold you over.*" How do you feel about this restaurant now? Might you go back? Most people will.

It's the same thing for communication. If something goes wrong – you slip and stereotype or you say something offensive – you can choose to ignore it or you can take action to recover from your mistake. Like Service Recovery, if you do it well and with sincerity, you can defuse tension, reestablish trust with your listeners, and build rapport for the entire group. It simply requires acknowledging what went wrong, apologizing, and fixing it.

The Gift of Feedback

Imagine you are making a presentation in a staff meeting when someone in the audience interrupts, perhaps angrily, pointing out that you made a bigoted statement. How would you feel? For most of us, this is uncomfortable – whether you are the presenter, the person speaking up, or simply attending the meeting.

As the communicator, the way you perceive this type of feedback sets the stage for your response. If you view feedback as an "attack," you might counter-attack, blame, or resent the person. If, however, you view the feedback as a "gift," your response will be different. You are more likely to receive it, say "*thanks*," and perhaps even use the gift graciously.

Feedback is good – Accept it! It is the gift of a second chance to communicate more effectively. Even if you don't like the feedback, accept it! Throwing a gift back at the person who gave it to you undermines your relationship with that person and with others who witnessed the exchange. Feedback, when well received, strengthens the bond between the feedback giver, others in the group, and you.

Communication Recovery – Six-Step Model

Communication Recovery allows you to acknowledge your mistake when things go wrong – when you have unintentionally demeaned, discounted, or excluded others. This gives you the chance to rebuild communication with your listener(s) and enhance your own credibility. Communication Recovery includes six quick steps and takes thirty seconds or less. It's relatively painless.

1. **Accept the Feedback** – Give some sign that you are open to the input, such as listening to and thanking the gift giver.

2. **Acknowledge Intent and Impact** – The most important thing here is to recognize the negative *impact* of your statement or behavior on the listener, regardless of your good intent.

3. **Apologize** – Say *"I'm sorry"* or *"I apologize,"* and do so sincerely.

4. **Ask Questions for Clarification** – If you don't understand the feedback you've been given, ask questions for greater clarity.

5. **Adjust / Change** – State or demonstrate what you will do differently. A clear sign that you've accepted the feedback is to not repeat the offense.

6. **Move Forward** – Recovery is a quick process. You don't need to linger. Move on once the listener is ready.

Of all of these, Accept the Feedback and Apologize may be the most powerful. In its simplest form, recovery sounds like this:

"Thanks for telling me. I'm sorry."
(Accept the Feedback, Apologize)

In the examples that follow, notice that the Communication Recovery steps are not necessarily chronological, and you don't have to include them all. Based on your comfort and the situation, use any or all of the six steps to recover from your mistake.

"Wow, I didn't even notice I was stereotyping age groups. Thanks for bringing that to my attention."
(Acknowledge Impact, Accept the Feedback)

"Thank you for pointing that out. I'm sorry I labeled you – that was not my intent."
(Accept the Feedback, Apologize, Acknowledge Intent and Impact)

"I meant that as a joke, but I can see now that what I said was inappropriate. Please forgive me."
(Acknowledge Intent and Impact, Apologize)

"Someone was kind enough to tell me on break that I've been talking about leaders only in the male gender and haven't referred to or acknowledged any women as leaders. Although that wasn't my intent, I can see how the examples I used did not include women's roles as leaders. I apologize for that and I'll be more sensitive in the future. And I hope you'll give me a chance to show that my commitment in developing leaders extends to both men and women."
(Acknowledge Intent and Impact, Apologize, Adjust / Change, Move Forward)

"Tony, I'm trying to understand, so stick with me. I want to be fair, but I don't see how what I said was unfair. Can you tell me more?"
(Accept the Feedback, Acknowledge Intent, Ask Questions for Clarification)

Seeking to better understand shows you are open to feedback and care about your listeners. After you've responded, you may also want to ask your gift giver if there is more she or he would like to talk about before moving on. Trust is built on two-way communication.

When *You* Know

The examples we've just covered assume that someone else is giving you the gift of feedback – and so you accept and open the gift. However, by paying attention to how others react nonverbally to your words and actions, you'll know (or at least sense) when you have stepped in it, even if no one else speaks up. You can still use the Communication Recovery steps – just omit the first step (Accept the Feedback).

"Oops, sorry – what I said was unfair. What I'm trying to say is…"
(Apologize, Acknowledge Impact, Adjust / Change)

"Whoa, I can't believe I just said that. Forgive me for stereotyping people. That was wrong. I'll try not to do that again."
(Acknowledge Impact, Apologize, Adjust / Change)

"Let's back up – That was pretty insensitive of me. Will you accept my apology?"
(Acknowledge Impact, Apologize)

Ask for Feedback

If something you've said evokes an unexpected verbal or nonverbal reaction, but you are not sure why, then ask. This demonstrates you care about how you affect others. And, you'll get educated in the process.

"I can tell I've said something wrong, but I don't know what. Can you help me understand?"
(Acknowledge Impact, Ask Questions for Clarification)

"What? Several of you just winced…obviously I've said something unacceptable…what is it?"
(Acknowledge Impact, Ask Questions for Clarification)

You can also leave open space in a conversation to allow for general feedback. You might ask: *"Any thoughts or feelings about what we just talked about?"*

The Apology That Isn't

Have you ever had someone apologize to you and you knew his or her heart wasn't in it? Then you know how it feels – empty. There's nothing gained by an apology that is insincere or that shifts the blame from the speaker to the listener – from the offender to the offended. These common non-apologies imply *"You're at fault."* Avoid these – they feel shallow, and they often up the tension, irritation, and mistrust others feel toward you. Some ineffective apologies are:

"I'm sorry you feel that way."

"I apologize if you are offended...perhaps you are being over-sensitive."

"I'm sorry you misunderstood."

"IF anything I said could be construed as offensive, then I apologize."

Acknowledging the impact of your own actions, rather than blaming the recipient, is more meaningful and effective. Notice the difference between the following phrases:

"I'm sorry you are offended," versus *"What I said was offensive – I'm sorry."*

"You are too sensitive," versus *"I was insensitive."*

Other Pitfalls to Avoid

Refusing the Gift of Feedback

When you receive feedback about the negative impact of your words, you have a golden opportunity to make it right. Refuse the gift and your opportunity to recover the listener's trust is lost. Refusing the feedback sounds something like this: *"I'm sorry you feel that way. I think others would agree with me that...,"* or more bluntly *"You're wrong"* or *"That's not true."* It's just as easy, and more powerful, to say, *"Wow, I didn't realize that. Thanks."*

Wallowing in Your Own Good Intent

This is a common mistake – spending all your Communication Recovery time and energy in justifying your own good reasons for what you said. If you want to acknowledge your good intent, make it short. The listener has received the negative impact of your words, and this is what should be addressed. You could say,

"I'm sorry I said that. I meant it to be funny, but I see it wasn't and that I embarrassed people."

Promising the Impossible

Be careful about saying *"I'll never stereotype again."* That's not very realistic. Better to say *"I'll try not to stereotype again … please tell me if you catch me making that same mistake."*

Repeating the Offense

An important step of Communication Recovery is to "Adjust / Change." In other words, it is essential to commit to a change, and then to actually change your behavior. Knowingly repeating the offense shows you have not received the gift and do not intend to in the future. This negates any recovery efforts. Here are examples of repeating the offense.

A colleague just asked you not to call her *"honey."* You reply, *"Lighten up, sweetie, I didn't mean anything by it."*

You just stereotyped long-term employees and when called on it, respond, *"I don't mean that 'old timers' aren't valuable to our team. They are; it's just that they don't generate NEW ideas."*

It's Not Always Pretty

You may receive a gift that is elegantly wrapped in kindness or eloquence. Other times the gift may be wrapped in sarcasm, anger, or inarticulate words. It's still a gift. Accept it.

Likewise, your recovery may be awkward and the words may not be perfect. That's OK too. Your sincere efforts will usually be appreciated.

Sometimes You Want to Open the Gift in Private

Occasionally you will receive feedback that you feel is best to deal with at a later time. You can still use Communication Recovery to accept the feedback, acknowledge the giver, and commit to follow up.

For instance, imagine you are leading a group discussion and a participant says that you or your company discriminates against a group of people. Rather than asking questions to further explore the situation in the large group, your response may be more like this:

Accept: *"Thank you for that feedback. What you are saying is very important to me."*

Acknowledge Intent, Adjust / Change, Move Forward: *"Our intent is to provide a nondiscriminatory workplace for every employee, and so I want to follow up with you to ensure that happens. Let's talk further following our group discussion."*

Notice that you have emphasized *intent* here rather than *impact*. (Careful investigation is required to better understand whether discrimination has in fact occurred.) You have committed to follow up here and *must* do so. In fact, if you are a member of management, you have a legal duty to act in this situation. Following the meeting, you could ask this participant to meet with you and the Human Resources representative the next day to ensure all concerns are addressed. Involve your HR professional immediately, who will help you to respond appropriately to this feedback.

Summary

"Oops! I shouldn't have said that." You probably say or think this at least once in a while. If you are like most people who communicate frequently and spontaneously, sooner or later you end up with your foot in your mouth.

That's what Communication Recovery is all about. When you have unintentionally demeaned, stereotyped, or otherwise discounted or excluded others, you can use the Communication Recovery process to rebuild trust with listeners. It allows you to acknowledge, correct, and move past the communication static and get back to the intended message.

Remember that Communication Recovery involves six quick steps:

1. Accept the Feedback

2. Acknowledge Intent and Impact

3. Apologize

4. Ask Questions for Clarification

5. Adjust / Change

6. Move Forward

It's most effective to apologize immediately when things go wrong. Your sincerity will help clear the air and allow everyone, including you, to be more comfortable. However, if something you've said in the past still bothers you, it's better late than never. You can use this process to correct something you said yesterday, last week, last month, or even last year.

Just one

person taking

action can

inspire others

to do the

same.

Chapter Three

Speaking Up Against Bias

Without Blame or Guilt

"We will have to repent in this generation

not merely for the hateful words and

actions of the bad people but for the appalling

silence of the good people."

– Martin Luther King, Jr.

Why We Can't Wait, Letter From Birmingham Jail

What do you do if someone you care about is the target of demeaning stereotypes? Do you speak up when negative jokes or statements affect your team members or customers? What if you are being demeaned or stereotyped? This is one of the more difficult skills for people – knowing how to address others' comments or jokes that are biased, demeaning, or stereotypical.

Silent Collusion

Many people say they want to speak up but don't because of discomfort or fear of saying the wrong thing. Unfortunately, staying silent in the face of demeaning comments, stereotypes, or bias allows these attitudes and behaviors to thrive. This undermines our ability to create a respectful and productive workplace for everyone.

For some, saying nothing has a high personal cost. They replay the scene in their minds: *"I could have said...,"* *"I should have said...,"* *"Why didn't I speak up?"* Failure to speak up and confront issues can result in a huge drain of mental energy.

Why not redirect this energy to effectively respond next time? It will change the direction of the immediate conversation. It will set a respectful tone for the whole group and affect group dynamics in the future. Most importantly, you'll know you took action instead of staying silent.

Scenario: Speaking Up

I was at a party, relaxed, enjoying myself when the joke telling began: *"There were three _____ who went to the..."* The joke progressed. It was clearly demeaning to a group of people.

The face of my close friend and colleague popped into my mind – he is a member of the group being debased. Two different voices – the proverbial angel and devil on my shoulder – filled my head.

> *"Leslie, say something! You know you don't support this."*

> *"Relax, it's a party! Have fun...lighten up. People won't like you if you can't take a joke."*

> *"Speak up, you coward! You can't talk about valuing diversity all day at work and then stereotype people for entertainment at night. Be true to yourself."*

In those long seconds while I twitched and struggled with what to do, the disk jockey, who was sitting with us on break, simply said, *"Whoa! I'm not going there. I think I'd rather get something to drink."* He got up and walked across the room. I hopped up and followed him: *"Great idea!"*

I'll never forget what happened next. Others in the group joined us at the bar, leaving only two people to hear the joke's punch line. I was amazed. Few of us wanted to hear the joke, but we went along anyway. It took just *one voice* – one person casually speaking up against disrespect – to shift the entire conversation.

Who Can Do It?

Anyone can speak up in the face of demeaning comments. You don't have to be the boss or have authority. And, you don't have to be a brilliant communicator. Fact is, a simple phrase or question on your part could turn the conversation from destructive to productive.

However, if you *are* the boss, you *know* that your staff looks to you to set the example. Whenever something happens in your team that demeans an individual or diminishes group cohesiveness, all eyes rest on you. Your behaviors demonstrate "how things are around here." You are the role model others follow.

Regardless of your position, ask yourself how often you speak up on behalf of respectful treatment. How did you personally respond the last time you witnessed someone being treated with disrespect? Did you laugh or contribute? If so, you condoned and, in effect, reinforced the discounting and disrespect. Perhaps you looked or walked away, embarrassed, thinking, *"I can't believe what I just heard."* If so, why did you remain silent when you could have been a friend or advocate?

Ally Behavior

Hopefully you intervened. This is called "ally behavior" – speaking up on behalf of someone else. Sometimes, as a bystander, you have more power to influence change than does the targeted person, who may not be present, or may feel powerless to speak up, or may be stunned into silence. It isn't always easy to be the first to speak up, but it's the right thing to do. Just one person taking action can inspire others to do the same. Think of the disc jockey and how his sole voice made a difference.

What if It's Too Risky?

In the workplace, people say that often the person to whom they would like to give feedback is the boss or a senior manager in the organization. Therefore, they feel it's too risky to speak up. While I'm not encouraging any career-limiting decisions on your part, there are low-risk ways to express your concerns. You can speak to the person in private. You can call on a senior-level ally to help you. And, you can use one or more of the following feedback tools.

Twelve Techniques for Taking Action Without Blame or Guilt

Each of these techniques demonstrates an effective way to address stereotypes, bias, or discounting. Each allows you to "pause" the conversation or interrupt the behavior in a way that is respectful. Some techniques are simple and require very little energy, skill, or courage on your part. Others are more complex. You can use them in public or in private, in "real time" or after the fact, on behalf of yourself or as an ally for someone else. You wouldn't want to utilize all twelve techniques at once – that would be overkill. But you can choose one or several of them based on the context and your energy, comfort, and skill level.

A critical point – notice that none of these approaches attacks or insults the person who just said something biased or demeaning. Spitting out blame: *"You're a racist, homophobe, Neanderthal"* or exerting your weight and saying *"That's inappropriate – I want to see you in my office right now"* just doesn't work. Yes, you might shut people up, at least in your presence, but that's not helpful in the long run. The goal is to give feedback on the behavior in a manner that opens up conversation and does not diminish an individual or destroy group dynamics. Giving the gift of feedback doesn't have to be costly for anyone involved – for the giver or the recipient. Here's how to do it.

1) Assume Good Intent / Explain Impact

So how do you speak up against stereotypes or discounting comments without putting someone down? It's all in how you approach it. The key is to assume good intent; assume the other person is a decent human being. When you assume the best, there is no need to blame or insult the person who just said something biased or demeaning. There are effective ways to speak up without pouncing on someone, such as, *"I know you mean well but that really bothers me."*

Notice that there are two parts to this technique. The first half acknowledges the other person's positive intentions. The second half describes the negative results of the statement or behavior. These phrases illustrate 'Assume Good Intent / Explain Impact.'

"I'm sure you meant that to be funny, but that stereotype is no joke. Unfortunately, some people actually believe that."

"Hey, I know we're all just kidding around, but let's think about the impact of those types of jokes in the workplace."

"I really appreciate that you are trying to help me. But think about it — protecting me because of my gender takes away my chance to learn and gain experience."

"Kim, everyone knows how committed you are to the success of this team. Did you realize that something you have been doing is undermining us? Can I give you my perspective?"

"Chris, I know you wouldn't discriminate on purpose — but your decision could result in disparate impact. Can we look more closely at this?"

This technique is presented first because assuming good intent on the other person's part is the key to providing non-blaming feedback. Others are more likely to receive your gift of feedback if it is not wrapped in blame, anger, or sarcasm.

Assuming good intent also leaves you open to the possibility that an apparently biased word or deed was, in fact, not based in bias. Perhaps the person had poor information or made a naïve mistake. Or perhaps you heard this person incorrectly. It does happen. So, regardless of the feedback technique you choose, approach the person who has been offensive, demeaning, or discriminatory as *if* he or she did not intend harm.

The remaining techniques begin with those that are easiest. As you continue through the list, you will find more complex ways to give feedback, which require more energy and skill. It's best to have a repertoire of ways to give feedback so that you can choose what's right for you in any situation.

2) Say "Ouch!"

"*Ouch!*" is an acceptable four-letter word that communicates a lot with little effort. It says, "Your words had a negative impact on me." It's similar to what you might say if someone steps on your toes.

A more advanced use of "*Ouch!*" is to explain how the words or behavior affected you. For example, "*Ouch! That stereotype hurts. Let me tell you what that behavior really means in my culture.*" However, if you don't have the composure or desire at the moment to educate others, "*Ouch!*" by itself is still a good feedback tool.

3) Rephrase

With this subtle technique, you do not directly point out the language that was demeaning. Rather, you restate it in a more inclusive way when the opportunity arises. This is helpful when you do not want to interrupt the flow of conversation, yet you want to leave more inclusive language in people's minds. For example, someone comments, *"I'm not prejudiced against colored people. I just don't have any colored friends."* Without directly addressing the term "colored," which is outdated and perceived by many as bigoted, you could respond: *"I'm glad to hear you are not prejudiced against black people. What has happened in your life that has kept you from having African-American friends?"* This allows you to delve deeper into this topic without sidetracking the focus of the discussion. You can always come back later and talk about more appropriate and respectful word choices.

Another time you might want to rephrase with more equitable language is when one group is set up as the norm, and everyone else is positioned as the exceptions or 'non-norm,' such as in the phrase *"Both Christians and Non-Christians attended the ceremony."* You could rephrase this as: *"People of many faiths attended the ceremony"* or *"Among those who attended the ceremony were Muslims, Jews, Christians, and others."*

4) Ask a Question

This is an easy, low-risk, highly effective tool that everyone can use. You can change the outcome of a situation through the use of a non-blaming question. Some generic questions include:

"What do you mean, Bobbie?"
"What are you saying?"
"I don't think I heard you correctly. What did you say?"
"What is it that leads you to say that?"

Generic questions can be practiced in advance and used frequently. They must be sincere, open-ended questions. Refrain from questions that entrap or judge, such as *"Why in the world would you make such an offensive statement?"*

A more advanced skill is to ask specific questions based on the particular situation. One way to do this is to Repeat and Question.

5) Repeat and Question

Sometimes people don't realize what they've said. Repeating and questioning gives them a chance to reexamine and to perhaps recover. At other times, individuals communicate negative stereotypes or statements without directly saying them. This technique can help surface unspoken assumptions.

To spotlight a word or statement, you can repeat it verbatim.
"What do you mean, Bobbie, when you say, 'Isn't that just like a _____?' "

You can also paraphrase what you think you are hearing.
"It sounds like you are saying that Alan is too old to learn the computer. Is that what you mean?"

"Can we go back to what you said a few minutes ago? You mentioned immigration and the increase in crime in the same sentence. Are you suggesting that these two are linked?"

A word of caution – If the comment is hateful or highly offensive, you may choose not to repeat it verbatim. Simply paraphrasing or asking generic questions (Technique 4) may be a more respectful, lower-risk approach.

6) Interrupt and Redirect

Interrupting and redirecting changes the direction of the conversation abruptly, without necessarily soliciting further discussion. Imagine someone makes a slur or begins a joke that you suspect will be derogatory, such as *"How many _____ does it take to...?"* What do you do? Playfully interrupting with *"Whoa, let's not go there!"* or *"Danger! Quicksand ahead!"* opens up two possibilities. The joke-teller has the chance to change directions. If that doesn't happen, you have the opportunity to walk away. You can easily remove yourself from the situation without condoning, through silence, the disparaging remarks.

Here's an example of an assumption or stereotype that could result in an unfair, and possibly discriminatory, decision. During a hiring decision, a colleague says: *"The baby boomers aren't going to have the level of tech savvy we need. We need to recruit young kids right out of school."* To interrupt and redirect, you could say: *"Let's not assume that all young people will have the computer skills we need and that others will not. Let's test each person's skills and then make our decisions based on the results."*

Notice that in this case, you are combining several techniques – specifically naming the assumption (Technique 8), and then interrupting and redirecting.

7) Appeal to Empathy

Appealing to empathy (*How would you feel...? How do you think he feels...?*) is a technique that works well with people who *have* empathy. Not everyone does. However, even with empathy, you can't always put yourself in someone else's shoes. Fully understanding the cumulative impact of persistent denigration or discrimination may be difficult for those who have not personally experienced it. Given that, when you appeal to empathy, consider parallel ways someone might understand. For example, *"Sarah, remember how frustrated you were when Brenda dismissed your ideas because you were new here? Now it seems as though you are doing the same thing to Bruno simply because he has an accent. How do you think he feels?"*

8) Name It

In this response, you specifically identify, by name, what is happening. This spotlights the communication in question. Notice that this technique can be light-hearted or more serious, depending on the situation and the tone of voice.

"Now THAT would be a <u>stereotype</u>!"
"Do you believe that <u>stereotype</u>?"
"Time out – no '<u>dissing</u>' each other."
"What are our underlying <u>assumptions</u> here?"

9 & 10) Seek Contradictions / Make It Individual

Here are two different techniques that accomplish the same goal – breaking through the thought process of clumping people together in stereotypes. Both approaches reveal that while a certain behavior or characteristic may be true of an *individual*, it is not true of *everyone* in a group. You can use these techniques together or separately.

Stereotypical Statement: *"Management doesn't care about us."*
Seek Contradictions: *"Don't you know any supervisors or managers who DO care?"*
Make It Individual: *"Which manager are you referring to?"*

Stereotypical Statement: *"These young kids are slackers."*

Seek Contradictions: *"I think we have some great young employees. What about Damien and Kendra – they're both great."*

Make It Individual: *"Do you mean all young people or someone in particular?"*

Stereotypical Statement: *"Immigrants don't even try to speak English."*

Seek Contradictions: *"Actually, I've met dozens of immigrants who have learned English or are trying to learn it. It's not an easy task."*

Make It Individual: *"Is there someone in particular you weren't able to communicate with? You sound frustrated."*

11) Broaden to Universal Human Behavior

Next time someone attributes a trait to one particular group, consider broadening the description to universal human behavior. In other words, try to show that it is a human trait, not limited to the stereotyped group.

Stereotype: *"Teenagers can't be trusted."*

Broaden: *"I don't think that's an age thing. Do you know any people in their 40s or 50s who aren't trustworthy?"*

Stereotype: *"Men are good leaders."*

Broaden: *"Yes, some men are. But I think leadership is broader than that. I know some women who are pretty good leaders too…and some men who aren't."*

12) Use the "I" Voice / Classic Feedback Process

The last technique for giving feedback on demeaning, stereotypical, or discounting behavior is the classic feedback process. While feedback models vary, the key elements include: objectively describe the SITUATION and the BEHAVIOR you observed, and give feedback on the IMPACT using the 'I' voice. In its simplest form, it sounds like: *"When you made the 'fat' comment in the meeting, I felt humiliated."*

This is a great tool for more in-depth feedback. Using the classic feedback process, you would say:

"Sal, remember yesterday in the quarterly staff meeting when you introduced our new sales rep. You said, 'We finally got an African American AND a female on our staff – we've been trying for a long time to be more diverse.' You didn't say anything about Tanya's great experience and qualifications.

What I noticed, Sal, is that she seemed very uncomfortable with your introduction. To me, it felt like you were saying that that's why you hired Tanya – for her race and gender, not for her talent. I think that had a negative effect on her."

While the above feedback works, it would be even stronger by adding what we already know about assuming good intent and asking questions to open up the conversation. It would sound more like this:

"Sal, remember yesterday in the quarterly staff meeting when you introduced our new sales rep. You said, 'We finally got an African American AND a female on our staff – we've been trying for a long time to be more diverse.' You didn't say anything about Tanya's great experience and qualifications.

I'm sure you meant to give Tanya a warm, enthusiastic welcome, but what I noticed, Sal, is that she seemed very uncomfortable with your introduction. To me, it felt like you were saying that that's why you hired Tanya – for her race and gender, not for her talent.

Is that what you meant?
How do you think that's going to affect Tanya and others' perceptions of her qualifications?
Is there anything else you want to say to Tanya or to the other staff members?

Thanks, Sal."

This may require more time than some of the previous techniques we've explored, but it's great for two-way conversation and coaching. Sal now has the opportunity to practice Communication Recovery and to support Tanya's success in her new role.

Summary

Whenever you witness non-inclusive, discounting, or discriminatory words and actions, you have a choice. You can choose to remain silent, which allows these behaviors to thrive. Or you can speak up on behalf of respect.

Using the techniques in this chapter enhances your ability to interrupt bias, stereo-types, or other demeaning messages. To get comfortable, practice all twelve. Then choose the one – or ones – that works best in any situation. You can give feedback in private or in public. When you speak up immediately, everyone learns. At times, you or the recipient will be more comfortable with a private conversation – that's OK too.

Regardless of the techniques you use, always assume good intent. It will take the blame out of your voice and the defensiveness out of the other person. Remember, the twelve techniques are:

1. Assume Good Intent / Explain Impact
2. Say "Ouch!"
3. Rephrase
4. Ask a Question
5. Repeat and Question
6. Interrupt and Redirect
7. Appeal to Empathy
8. Name It
9. Seek Contradictions
10. Make It Individual
11. Broaden to Universal Human Behavior
12. Use the "I" Voice / Classic Feedback Process

Anyone can use these skills. So, go ahead; Say *"Ouch!"* when it hurts.

Chapter Four

Planning for Inclusion

"When someone with the authority of

a teacher, say, describes the world and you

are not in it, there is a moment of psychic

disequilibrium, as if you looked into a

mirror and saw nothing."

– Adrienne Rich

Blood, Bread, and Poetry

Most of the time, communication is informal and spontaneous, with little advance thought or planning. There are times, however, when you communicate through more organized venues or as a spokesperson for your team or organization. In these circumstances, you should plan in *advance* how you will communicate respect and inclusion for *all* audience members. It will enhance your ability to design and deliver a static-free message that reaches your intended audience.

Scenario: Unintended Message

I once unknowingly scheduled a "Valuing Diversity" workshop on an important Jewish holiday, which excluded a portion of the team's employees. That action alone spoke much louder than – and in contradiction to – anything I said about inclusion or valuing differences during the training. Since that time, I always check a multicultural calendar before scheduling events.

For easy use, the twenty-seven suggestions in this chapter are organized into a checklist. They cover not only the spoken content of the message, but also the context within which the message is delivered. This includes the environment, the meeting logistics, communication methodology, the graphics, and audience diversity. As you read, focus on the suggestions that will help you in your particular communication role – whether you share information in staff meetings, lead training sessions, communicate at employee or customer events, or work in marketing, sales, public relations, communications, or community outreach.

Advance Planning Checklist: Communicating Respect and Inclusion

General Planning

- Learn about audience demographics such as age, origin, work experience, disabilities, and languages spoken.

- If you are using an event coordinator, select someone with the willingness to accommodate diverse needs (e.g., diet, translation, accessibility).

Scheduling

- Use a multicultural calendar to avoid scheduling events on important ethnic or religious holidays.

- Allot sufficient time for participants to complete pre- and post-program assignments while still observing ethnic or religious holidays and family responsibilities.

Advance Communication

- Solicit information on attendees' requests / requirements regarding access, learning accommodations, or dietary needs.

- Provide multiple ways for people to communicate with you (e.g., telephone, Telecommunications Device for the Deaf (TDD), fax, e-mail, or in person).

- Distribute meeting agendas and other written information in advance of your session. This enables full participation for individuals who are more comfortable contributing ideas if they have prepared their thoughts in advance (i.e., based on behavioral style, language skills, and cultural norms).

Universal Access

- Choose a location that is physically accessible and socially comfortable for all participants (e.g., don't hold a team meeting at a restaurant where employees are scantily clad). Complete an environmental scan, looking for accessibility as well as subtle nonverbal messages that are inclusive or exclusive.

- Select food and refreshments that are acceptable to a broad audience base (e.g., include drinks that contain no alcohol or caffeine and have access to food that is vegetarian or adheres to religious guidelines, such as kosher or halal foods).

- Arrange the meeting room so that aisles and walkways between tables are wide enough for individuals using wheelchairs. Ensure appropriate seating for people who need an unobstructed view of the speaker, such as individuals with hearing impairments.

- Check availability of audio-visual materials in various formats (e.g., written audio scripts, closed-captioned videos, large print). Become familiar with the audio-visual equipment so that you can use the closed-caption format if needed.

Content Development / Methodology

- Complete a bias check on all written materials and speech notes.

- Select visual aids and graphics that depict human diversity and that avoid stereotypical portrayals.

- Use quotes, stories, examples, analogies, and visuals that depict a broad range of people as role models.

- For idea generation or other audience participation, include various methodologies, such as individual work, small group discussion, and both verbal and written input. Avoid overuse of brainstorming, which may exclude some people based on behavioral style, cultural norms, or language skills.

- Design alternate methodologies so that all members can participate and receive the same learning or outcome (e.g., alternate activity for a ropes course, activities geared toward all learning styles).

- Add a question to your meeting evaluation form on whether attendees felt included and respected.

Multilingual Preparations
- Engage interpreters, if needed, including sign language interpreters. Brief presenters on the effective use of interpreters.

- Translate written materials, if needed.

Entertainment and Recreation
- Select entertainment or recreation options that represent the broad diversity of the audience (e.g., age, culture, language, abilities).

- Ensure activities do not stereotype any group (e.g., don't assume that all men play golf and all women want to shop).

Religious and Spiritual Needs
- For community events involving prayer, consider inviting clerics from various religions to lead the invocation. Utilize an ecumenical prayer that acknowledges all faiths. Respect the rights of those who choose not to participate.

- Inform event staff where there are quiet rooms that can be used for prayer and restrooms or showers for ritual cleansing.

- Schedule breaks that will enable individuals to meet their religious or spiritual requirements.

- If religious symbolism will be present, include multiple faiths (e.g., Christmas tree, menorah, and other symbols of the season).

Facilitation Team

- Ensure company representatives and guest presenters represent a cross section of the organization and the diversity within.

- Discuss, in advance, your commitment to bias-free and inclusive communication with all invited speakers.

Summary

You may have heard the saying *"People don't care how much you know until they know how much you care."* It's true. So when you are planning communication, consider the various ways you can send the message that all listeners are valued. You can proactively create an atmosphere where your message can be heard by many different people. This is particularly important when you are communicating on behalf of your organization or when you are planning team or company gatherings.

So, take some extra time to plan in advance for a diverse range of listeners. It's worth it – people have different learning styles, different physical abilities, different cultures and languages, different needs and interests. This way, everyone benefits.

Many factors contribute to the message of inclusion, from the bias-free language and content you choose, to the facilitators you select and the examples you cite, to the accessibility of the location. It is the cumulative impact of these decisions that will determine your communication success.

Closing Thoughts

"I am only one; but still I am one.

I cannot do everything,

but still I can do something.

I will not refuse to do the something I can do."

– Helen Keller

I'd like to say *"We're finished – now that you've read this book, the hard work is done. That's everything you need to know or do to achieve respectful, bias-free communication."* But, I can't. The real work begins now. Where will you go from here? Which ideas, concepts, models, and techniques will you incorporate to enhance your communication?

If you have a plan in place, that's great! If you don't, allow me to suggest the following path.

Look Inward

Awareness is the first step to positive change. Continue to search within yourself to identify your own biases. Pay attention, on an ongoing basis, to the ways you may communicate bias or exclusion. Once you have this at a conscious level, you can make conscious decisions. Then you can question and interrupt, rather than perpetuate bias.

Learn From Your Mistakes

Consider an event that has already happened – one of those times you unintentionally demeaned someone or said something you regretted. Using the six-step Communication Recovery Model, practice what you would say today if this happened again. How would you clear the air? If you want, and if you have the option available, you can still go to that person and apologize. Or, simply use the situation as a learning experience. And if you once again find your foot in your mouth in the future, apologize in the moment. That will make it easier on everyone.

Speak Up! Interrupt! Intervene!

When you next encounter biased behavior or words – and you won't have to wait long – say something! Have at least two generic questions in your pocket that will allow you to "pause" the situation and open up dialogue. Plus, get comfortable with several of the other techniques and use them. Always assume the other person is a decent human being and did not intend harm. This way, you can speak up against biased words and behaviors in a way that doesn't blame or cause guilt.

Plan Ahead

Don't leave bias-free and inclusive communication to chance. Set aside time to complete the Advance Planning Checklist, on pages 64-67, before you stand in front of your next audience. Planning in advance will result in fewer unanticipated disruptions to your message.

Learn From Others

Find good role models you can learn from – colleagues, friends, or family members with exceptional communication skills who don't shy away from difficult conversations. Look for individuals who are respectful and bias-free in their communication. Notice what they do. Follow their lead. Ask for their advice. There are other ways, too, to continue your learning. Attend a workshop or read up on bias reduction. Ask others for feedback on the impact of your communication. If you are open to receive the gift, gifts will be given.

Listen With Kindness

Much of this book focuses on the messages you *send*. It's just as important to *receive* messages with respect and compassion. Allow others their mistakes…we all make them. Don't search out bias or non-inclusion just for the chance to pounce on or correct someone. Give others the benefit of the doubt. And – it's worth repeating – always, always assume good intent!

Doing these things will not guarantee that you will communicate in ways that are respectful, inclusive, and free of bias 100% of the time. We're human after all, and we make mistakes. (That's what Communication Recovery is all about.) You will be more likely, however, to reduce communication static, gain your listener's ear, heart, and confidence, and open the door to meaningful dialogue. You will also respond more effectively in the face of bias or other discounting behaviors. This allows you to continue to build your credibility as a communicator and as a person, and to build a workplace where *all* people feel included, respected, and able to do their best work.

Where

will you

go from

here?

"But where was I to start?

The world is so vast.

I shall start with the country

I know best, my own.

But my country is so very large.

I had better start with my town.

But my town, too, is large.

I had best start with my street.

No: my home. No: my family.

Never mind, I shall start with myself."

– Elie Wiesel

Souls on Fire

About the Author

Leslie Aguilar is president of International Training and Development. She is recognized as an innovative speaker, facilitator, and curriculum developer in the areas of Diversity and Cultural Competence. Leslie has developed three diversity / inclusion instruments: *Diversity Competencies Assessment,*™ *Diversity Leadership 360°,*™ and *DiversiScan.*™ She coauthored *Multicultural Customer Service: Providing Outstanding Service Across Cultures* (McGraw Hill, 1996) and coproduced the video-based training program *Service Savvy: Providing Outstanding Service in a Diverse World* in 2004.

Leslie currently serves on the National Workplace Diversity Special Expertise Panel for the Society for Human Resource Management. She is past-chair of the Central Florida Diversity Council - American Society for Training and Development. Leslie was educated in foreign languages in Mexico, Spain, France, Switzerland, and the U.S., and was a Rotary International Scholar.

Leslie welcomes your feedback and questions on this book and topic. You can reach her at www.TheDiversityCenter.com.

About the Publisher

Since 1977, The WALK THE TALK® Company has helped organizations and individuals, worldwide, achieve success through Ethical Leadership and Values-Based practices. Our mission is both simple and straightforward: to provide you and your organization with high-impact resources for your personal and professional success!

We specialize in:

◆ How-To Handbooks and Support Materials

◆ Inspirational Gift Books and Movies

◆ Comprehensive Video Training Programs

◆ Do-It-Yourself Training Resources

◆ 360 Degree Feedback Processes

◆ The Popular *212° the extra degree, Santa's Leadership Secrets* and *Start Right…Stay Right* Product Lines
…and much more!

**To order additional copies of this high-impact book
or to learn more about our full-range of resources, visit
www.walkthetalk.com**

Available Now!

Ouch! That Stereotype Hurts Video Training Program!

OUCH! THAT STEREOTYPE HURTS is a new video program for training in Diversity & Inclusion, Communication, Teamwork and Leadership.

OUCH! Learning Objectives:

◆ Understand the impact of stereotypes and biased statements, even when casually said.

◆ Identify the most common reasons people sit silent in the face of bias and stereotypes.

◆ Enhance skills for speaking up against stereotypes without blame or guilt.

The OUCH! package includes:

◆ 14-minute video (VHS or DVD)

◆ Leader's Guide and PowerPoint presentation (CD)

◆ 1 copy of the book, **OUCH!** *That Stereotype Hurts*

◆ 10 reminder cards with the **OUCH!** Techniques

For pricing information and a free online preview, visit www.walkthetalk.com

Also consider these other powerful WALK THE TALK® Resources!

The Manager's Communication Handbook

This powerful handbook will allow you to connect with employees and create understanding, support, and acceptance crucial to your individual and organizational success. $9.95

Walk Awhile in MY Shoes

The revolutionary two-handbooks-in-one that helps breakdown "us vs. them" beliefs and behaviors – and encourages new levels of trust, teamwork, and focuses on common goals. $9.95

Ethics4Everyone

Unique and powerful resource for employees at ALL levels. It provides practical information to guide individual actions, decisions, and daily behaviors. When it comes to ethics, everyone is responsible ... everything counts! $9.95

Walking The Talk Together

Focusing on shared responsibility, this easy-to-read handbook pinpoints the ten critical behaviors that everyone must adopt in order to build a team-oriented environment of trust, commitment, and integrity. $9.95

Start Right...Stay Right

Every employee's straight-talk guide to personal responsibility and job success. Focusing on attitudes and behaviors, this best-seller is a "must read" for seasoned employees as well as new staff additions. $9.95

ORDER FORM

Have questions? Need assistance? Call 1.888.822.9255

 Please send me additional copies of OUCH! THAT STEREOTYPE HURTS

1-24 copies: $12.95 ea.   25-99 copies: $11.95 ea.   100-499 copies: $10.95 ea.   500+ copies: *please call **1.888.822.9255***

OUCH! THAT STEREOTYPE HURTS
Communicating Respectfully in a Diverse World ____copies   X $_____   = $_____

Additional Resources From WALK THE TALK

Ouch! That Stereotype Hurts Video Training Program   ____copies X $ 695.00 = $_____
The Manager's Communication Handbook   ____copies X $ 9.95 = $_____
Walk Awhile in MY Shoes   ____copies X $ 9.95 = $_____
Ethics4Everyone   ____copies X $ 9.95 = $_____
Walking The Talk Together   ____copies X $ 9.95 = $_____
Start Right...Stay Right   ____copies X $ 9.95 = $_____

Product Total	$_____
*Shipping & Handling	$_____
Subtotal	$_____
Sales Tax:	
TX Sales Tax – 8.25%	$_____
CA Sales/Use Tax	$_____
TOTAL (U.S. Dollars Only)	$_____

(Sales & Use Tax Collected on TX & CA Customers Only)

*Shipping and Handling Charges

No. of Items	1-4	5-9	10-24	25-49	50-99	100-199	200+
Total Shipping	$6.75	$10.95	$17.95	$26.95	$48.95	$84.95	$89.95+$0.25/book

Call 972.899.8300 for quote if outside continental U.S. Orders are shipped ground delivery 3-5 business days.
Next and 2nd business day delivery available – call 1.888.822.9255.

Name_____   Title _____

Organization _____

Shipping Address _____
No P.O. Boxes

City_____   State_____ Zip _____

Phone _____   Fax _____

E-Mail_____

Charge Your Order: ❑ MasterCard   ❑ Visa   ❑ American Express

Credit Card Number_____ Exp. _____

❑ Check Enclosed (Payable to: The WALK THE TALK Company)

❑ Please Invoice (Orders over $250 ONLY) P.O. # (required)_____

Prices effective July, 2007 are subject to change.

PHONE	ONLINE	MAIL
PHONE **1.888.822.9255** *or* 972.899.8300 M-F, 8:30 – 5:00 Central	**ONLINE** **www.walkthetalk.com** **FAX** **972.899.9291**	**MAIL** WALKTHETALK.COM 1100 Parker Square, Suite 250 Flower Mound, TX 75028